Creatures

Other poetry anthologies edited by
Lee Bennett Hopkins

Creatures

POEMS SELECTED BY
Lee Bennett Hopkins

ILLUSTRATED BY
Stella Ormai

HARCOURT BRACE JOVANOVICH, PUBLISHERS
SAN DIEGO   NEW YORK   LONDON

LIBRARY OF CONGRESS CATALOGING IN PUBLICATION DATA
Main entry under title:
Creatures.
Includes index.
SUMMARY: A collection of English and American
poems featuring a variety of magical and
supernatural creatures.
1. Children's poetry, American. 2. Children's
poetry, English. 3. Fantastic poetry, American.
4. Fantastic poetry, English. [1. Supernatural—
Poetry. 2. Monsters—Poetry. 3. American
poetry—Collections. 4. English
poetry—Collections]
I. Hopkins, Lee Bennett. II. Ormai, Stella, ill.
PS586.C74 1985 821'.008'0375 84-15698
ISBN 0-15-220875-5
ISBN 0-15-220876-3 (pbk.)

Printed and bound by South China Printing Company, Hong Kong

B C D E
A B C D E (pbk.)

HBJ

Every effort
has been made to trace the ownership
of all copyrighted material and to secure the
necessary permissions to reprint these selections.
In the event of any question arising as to the use
of any material, the editor and publisher, while
expressing regret for any inadvertent error, will
be happy to make the necessary correction
in future printings.

Thanks are due to the following for permission to
reprint the copyrighted materials listed in the
next column.

ATHENEUM PUBLISHERS, INC., for "Sea Fairies" from
8 A.M. Shadows by Patricia Hubbell. Copyright
© 1965 by Patricia Hubbell. Reprinted by
permission of Atheneum Publishers, an imprint of
Macmillan Company.

LAURA CECIL, LITERARY AGENT, for "The Old Wife and
the Ghost" from The Wandering Moon and Other
Poems by James Reeves (Puffin Books). Reprinted
by permission of the James Reeves Estate.

CURTIS BROWN, LTD., for "In the Pitch of the Night"
by Lee Bennett Hopkins. Copyright © 1979 by Lee
Bennett Hopkins. Used by permission of Curtis
Brown, Ltd.

GARRARD PUBLISHING COMPANY for "Troll Trick" by
B. J. Lee from Poetry of Witches, Elves and Goblins
by Leland B. Jacobs. Copyright 1970 by Leland B.
Jacobs. Reprinted by permission of Garrard
Publishing Company, Champaign, Illinois.

BARBARA M. HALES for "Do Fairies Like the Rain?"
Used by permission of the author, who controls all
rights.

HARPER & ROW, PUBLISHERS, INC., for "Knitted
Things" from Dogs & Dragons, Trees & Dreams by
Karla Kuskin. Copyright © 1962 by Karla Kuskin.
Reprinted by permission of Harper & Row,
Publishers, Inc.

FLORENCE PARRY HEIDE for "What's That?" Used by
permission of the author, who controls all rights.

MACMILLAN PUBLISHING COMPANY, INC., for excerpt
from "Song" and for "Witches' Song" from Summer
Green by Elizabeth Coatsworth. Copyright © 1948
by Macmillan Publishing Company, Inc., renewed
1976 by Elizabeth Coatsworth; "The Seven Ages of
Elf-Hood" from Poems by Rachel Field. Copyright
1926 by Macmillan Publishing Company, Inc.,
renewed 1954 by Arthur S. Pederson. Reprinted
by permission of Macmillan Publishing
Company, Inc.

MARIAN REINER for "Ghosts" from The Golden Hive
by Harry Behn. Copyright © 1957, 1962, 1966 by
Harry Behn; "The Gnome" from Windy Morning by
Harry Behn. Copyright 1953 by Harry Behn.
Copyright renewed 1981 by Alice Behn Goebel,
Pamela Behn Adams, Prescott Behn, and Peter
Behn. All rights reserved. "Bedtime Stories" from
See My Lovely Poison Ivy by Lilian Moore. Copyright
© 1975 by Lilian Moore. Reprinted by permission of
Marian Reiner for the authors.

VIKING PENGUIN, INC., and OLWYN HUGHES LITERARY
AGENCY for "The Dracula Vine" from Moon Whales
and Other Poems by Ted Hughes. Copyright © 1963,
1976 by Ted Hughes. Reprinted by permission of
Viking Penguin, Inc., and Olwyn Hughes Literary
Agency.

*For
Donald George Hopkins—
An Extraordinary One.
—L.B.H.*

Bedtime Stories

LILIAN MOORE

"Tell me a story,"
Says Witch's Child.

"About the Beast
So fierce and wild.

About a Ghost
That shrieks and groans.

A Skeleton
That rattles bones.

About a Monster
Crawly-creepy.

Something nice
To make me sleepy!"

Witches' Song

ELIZABETH COATSWORTH

Early, early, comes the dark,
something moves along the ditches.
Was that singing? Hark, oh, hark
to the chanting of the witches!

Come, sisters, come,
let us screech at the windows,
let us blow out the candles
and breathe on their hair,

we've shadowed the moon
and called up the night-wind,
the owl and the cat and the broom
will be there.

Let us turn their blood chill
with the sight of our faces,
let us touch them with fingers
both crooked and cold,

and then shrilly laughing
we'll be off to the hill tops
to frisk and to frolic
as always of old.

Did you hear them? Were they saying
scary things to shake the knees?
Or was that but breezes playing
in the dry and brittle trees?

Knitted Things

KARLA KUSKIN

There was a witch who knitted things:
Elephants and playground swings.
She knitted rain,
She knitted night,
But nothing really came out right.
The elephants had just one tusk
And night looked more
Like dawn or dusk.
The rain was snow
And when she tried
To knit an egg
It came out fried.
She knitted birds
With buttonholes
And twenty rubber butter rolls.
She knitted blue angora trees.
She purl stitched countless purple fleas.
She knitted a palace in need of a darn.
She knitted a battle and ran out of yarn.
She drew out a strand
Of her gleaming, green hair
And knitted a lawn
Till she just wasn't there.

Skeleton and Spirit

ANONYMOUS

A skeleton once in Khartoum
Asked a spirit up into his room;
    They spent the whole night
    In the eeriest fight
As to which should be frightened of whom!

Ghosts

HARRY BEHN

A cold and starry darkness moans
   And settles wide and still
Over a jumble of tumbled stones
   Dark on a darker hill.

An owl among those shadowy walls,
   Gray against the gray
Of ruins and brittle weeds, calls
   And soundless swoops away.

Rustling over scattered stones
   Dancers hover and sway,
Drifting among their own bones
   Like webs of the Milky Way.

The Old Wife and the Ghost

JAMES REEVES

There was an old wife and she lived all alone
    In a cottage not far from Hitchin:
And one bright night, by the full moon light,
    Comes a ghost right into her kitchen.

About that kitchen neat and clean
    The ghost goes pottering round.
But the poor old wife is deaf as a boot
    And so hears never a sound.

The ghost blows up the kitchen fire,
    As bold as bold can be;
He helps himself from the larder shelf,
    But never a sound hears she.

He blows on his hands to make them warm,
    And whistles aloud "Whee-hee!"
But still as a sack the old soul lies
    And never a sound hears she.

From corner to corner he runs about,
    And into the cupboard he peeps;
He rattles the door and bumps on the floor,
    But still the old wife sleeps.

Jangle and bang go the pots and pans,
    As he throws them all around;
And the plates and mugs and dishes and jugs,
    He flings them all to the ground.

Madly the ghost tears up and down
    And screams like a storm at sea;
And at last the old wife stirs in her bed—
    And it's "Drat those mice," says she.

Then the first cock crows and morning shows
    And the troublesome ghost's away.
But oh! what a pickle the poor wife sees
    When she gets up next day.

"Them's tidy big mice," the old wife thinks,
    And off she goes to Hitchin,
And a tidy big cat she fetches back
    To keep the mice from her kitchen.

Troll Trick

B. J. LEE

With many a scowl
And many a frown,
A troll pushed
Stones and boulders down.

The crashing sound
Made town folks wonder:
Is it a troll
Or is it thunder?

But hill folks knew.
When boulders roll,
It's always the trick
Of a terrible troll.

The Gnome

HARRY BEHN

I saw a gnome
As plain as plain
Sitting on top
Of a weathervane.

He was dressed like a crow
In silky black feathers,
And there he sat watching
All kinds of weathers.

He talked like a crow too,
Caw caw caw,
When he told me exactly
What he saw,

Snow to the north of him
Sun to the south,
And he spoke with a beaky
Kind of a mouth.

But he wasn't a crow,
That was plain as plain
'Cause crows never sit
On a weathervane.

What I saw was simply
A usual gnome
Looking things over
On his way home.

The Seven Ages of Elf-Hood

RACHEL FIELD

When an Elf is as old as a year and a minute
He can wear a cap with a feather in it.

By the time that he is two times two
He has a buckle for either shoe.

At twenty he is fine as a fiddle,
With a little brown belt to go round his middle.

When he's lived for fifty years or so
His coat may have buttons all in a row.

If past threescore and ten he's grown
Two pockets he has for his very own.

At eighty-two or three years old
They bulge and jingle with bits of gold.

But when he's a hundred and a day
He gets a little pipe to play.

Do Fairies Like the Rain?

BARBARA M. HALES

Do Fairies like a rainy day?
No! They hide and cry;
Their filmy wings—if they got wet
Would sag, and never fly.

Rain drops, rain drops
Leave the Fairies be!
Fall upon the Leprechaun
Or Mermaids in the sea.

Do Pixies like a rainy day
A-piping through the dell?
The Pixies must enjoy the rain;
That's when they weave their spell.

Rain drops, rain drops
Play a Pixie-tune.
But don't fall on the Fairies
In the Pink-and-Green Lagoon.

Do Giants like a rainy day?
Oh yes! It makes them shout!
They love the large and massive prints
Their huge boots hollow out.

Rain drops, rain drops,
Giants LOVE the rain.
But don't fall on the Fairies
Or they will all complain.

Sea Fairies

PATRICIA HUBBELL

Look in the caves at the edge of the sea
If you seek the fairies of spray,
They thrive in the dampness of sea and tide,
With conch for breakfast and lobsters to ride,
With gulls to fly and tides to boom
And the long, white, wandering waves to roam.
Look in the caves! Look in the caves!
When spray fairies hide they flee for caves!
They capture a starfish and fling him high
Till he hooks on the edge of the cloud-borne sky
And there he'll dry till they fetch him down,
The mischievous fairies that live in the foam,
The wayward, white-winged fairies of spray
That ride green lobsters out of the bay
Then float back in on a horseshoe crab,
Scamper and turn and dash for their caves,
Swept by the waves.
Look in the caves! Look in the caves!

FROM

The Mermaid

ALFRED, LORD TENNYSON

I

Who would be
A mermaid fair,
Singing alone,
Combing her hair
Under the sea,
In a golden curl
With a comb of pearl,
On a throne?

II

I would be a mermaid fair;
I would sing to myself the whole of the day;
With a comb of pearl I would comb my hair;
And still as I comb'd I would sing and say,
'Who is it loves me? who loves not me?'

FROM

Song

ELIZABETH COATSWORTH

"I like fish," said the Mermaid,
"and the sharp rustle of waves,
and the branching shapes of corals
that grow on seamen's graves,
I like the wetness and the depth and the silence,
I like green caves."

The Dracula Vine

TED HUGHES

People on the moon love a pet.
But there's only one pet you can get—
The Dracula Vine, a monstrous sight!
But the moon-people like it all right.

This pet looks like a climbing plant
Made from parts of elephant.
But each flower is a hippo's head
Endlessly gaping to be fed.

Now this pet eats everything—
Whatever you can shovel or fling.
It snaps up all your old cardboard boxes
Your empty cans and your stuffed foxes.

And wonder of wonders! The very flower
You have given something to devour
Sprouts on the spot a luscious kind of pear
Without pips, and you can eat it there.

So this is a useful pet
And loyal if well-treat.
But if you treat it badly
It will wander off sadly

Till somebody with more garbage than you
Gives its flowers something to do.

What's That?

FLORENCE PARRY HEIDE

What's that?
Who's there?
There's a great huge horrible *horrible*
creeping up the stair!
A huge big terrible *terrible*
with creepy crawly hair!
There's a ghastly grisly *ghastly*
with seven slimy eyes!
And flabby grabby tentacles
of a gigantic size!
He's crept into my room now,
he's leaning over me.
I wonder if he's thinking
how delicious I will be.

In the Pitch of the Night

LEE BENNETT HOPKINS

In the pitch of the night,
where there isn't a light,
comes a very bad rabbit
with a horrible habit
of filling my head
with dangers—

    wanting to take me
    through forests
    where strangers
    and ghoulies
    high in the trees
    try to leap out at me.

So I say,
"Listen here, rabbit,
I'm sick of your habit.
I've had enough
of your nightmarish fright.

My bed is *my* bed
not some rabbit-filled head
    of monsters and dragons
    and weird plants that bite!

Now get out of my room!
Go on your own way!
Sleep has to come
before
     night
         turns
             to
                day!''

Ghost Sounds

ANONYMOUS

When the moon
rides high,
up overhead—
and I am snug
and warm
in bed—
in the autumn dark
the ghosts move 'round,
making their
mournful,
moaning
sound.

I listen to know
when the ghosts
go by.
I hear a wail.
I hear a sigh.

But I can't quite tell
which I hear
the most—
the wind,
or the wail
or some passing
ghost.

FROM

An Old Cornish Litany

ANONYMOUS

From Ghoulies and Ghosties,
And long-leggity Beasties,
And all THINGS
That go BUMP in the night.
Good Lord, deliver us.

Index

OF AUTHORS, TITLES, AND FIRST LINES